Alan Greenspan:
An economic mastermind?

Mr. R. Naroharo

Dedicated to my wife and family.

CONTENTS

EXECUTIVE SUMMARY

Since many years he is an inspiration for many people all around the globe. You could say that he has led the USA - and as a result many other countries - through various economic crises, and has a certain charismatic authority, that if he speaks, you just want to listen to his words. His name?

Alan Greenspan.

Before becoming the chairman of the FED (Federal Reserve), he had his own economic consultancy firm, and served both President Ford and President Nixon in several councils. After retiring in 2006, he started again as a private advisor.

Although there is, and has been, some criticism about his economic approach, he still is an inspiration for many people around the world, and his way of thinking is still of great influence for some of the economic decisions made right now.

In this report one will find an in-depth investigation of his decisions, speeches, and work ethics. Next to that you will find a research and perhaps even scrutiny on his management style, and an analysis on his leadership capabilities.

At the end of the report, all pieces will fall into place, and we finally get an answer on the question: Is he a leader, a manager, or perhaps even both?

1 INTRODUCTION

Alan Greenspan is a logical positivist, a man fond of numbers, and later he sort of embraced objectivism philosophy. In order to research this kind of man best, it is probably best to start with the bare facts and numbers.

Pre-FED

From the very early beginning on, he had an above interest in numbers, and at an age of 10 he already used some sort of code to analyze baseball games back in 1936. He then also learned to divide, by calculating batting averages, using no calculator, as far as 3 decimals.[1]

Although he was good in numbers, he started off as a musician. After high school he went to *Juilliard*, which is *a performing arts conservatory* located in NYC. He studied there piano, saxophone and

---

[1] Greenspan, Alan (2007). The age of turbulence: adventures in a new world. p. 38

clarinet, and his mission for the future was to play in the military chapel. Though, faith decided otherwise, since he was rejected for military service because of a spot on his lungs.

He started playing in bands, and ensembles, and he even played along with the later legendary *Stanley Getz*. Further on, he played in the *Henry Jerome Orchestra*, where he was seen as an economic intellect, and soon he was doing the tax redemption for his fellow players.[2],[3]

In the autumn of 1945 he made, according to himself, one of the best judgments he ever made: he enrolled in the faculty of trade, accountancy and finance at University of NY, where he received only 2 B-, and for the rest of all the subjects, straight A+. He earned his Summa Cum Laude B.S., and two years later, in 1950, his M.A. degree in economics.

---

[2] Greenspan, Alan (2007). The age of turbulence: adventures in a new world. pp. 40-46
[3] Martin, Justin (2000). Greenspan, The man behind money. pp.11-13, 27-31

During his studies he worked at an Investment bank *Brown Brothers Harriman,* where he made seasonal adjustments, and made more detailed versions of the sales statistics reported by the FED.[4] At the end of his studies, he had the option to choose between 2 companies, an advertisement firm, and the NICB (*The National Industrial Conference Board).*

Although the ad firm paid significantly more (60 $/week against 45$/week), he decided to join the NICB, because he thought he could learn more over there.[5]After his M.A. degree, he went to Colombia University to pursue *advanced economics.* Though, soon he dropped out due to "cash-flow" problems.[6],[7]

---

[4] Greenspan, Alan (2007). The age of turbulence: adventures in a new world. pp. 49-50

[5]Greenspan, Alan (2007). The age of turbulence: adventures in a new world. pp. 50-51

[6]Greenspan, Alan (2007). The age of turbulence: adventures in a new world. pp. 53

[7]Martin, Justin (2000). Greenspan, The man behind money. pp. 27-31

Later on, he didn't had the time anymore to do his dissertation, because of the amount of work created by his firm.

In 1954 he started an economic consultant firm, named *"Townsend-Greenspan Co. Inc."* together with Bill Townsend. The firm started of pretty quickly, and soon very reputable companies, which were almost all listed in the fortune-500, were asking for his services. Amongst others, *Republic steel, Vanguard Group, and Mobil Oil*, were his clients.[8]

In these years, (50's-60's) the contact between him and Ayn Rand intensified. Ayn was a writer and philosopher, and one of the founders of the *"objectivism philosophy"* Her "Magnum Opus" is a book called *"Atlas Shrugged"*, which according to a research conducted by the Modern Library, is the most important novel of the 20th century.[9]

---

[8]Greenspan, Alan (2007). The age of turbulence: adventures in a new world. pp. 66-67
[9]Modern Library, http://www.modernlibrary.com/top-100/100-best-novels/

One of her other books, called *"the virtue of selfishness"* can be seen as the most import non-fiction novel of the 20th century.[10]

Here is where he was impressed by the objectivism, and he had great believe in *Ayn* and her philosophy. According to himself and the NY Times, he had weekly gatherings in her apartment, and was he one of the few, who had read the masterpieces before publishing, allowing him to contribute to the stories, or give criticism.[11],[12],[13],[14]

In the year 1968 he started to work on the presidential campaign of Richard Nixon. First for his view and speeches on economical topics, and later

[10] Modern Library, http://www.modernlibrary.com/top-100/100-best-nonfiction/

[11] NY Times, http://www.nytimes.com/2007/10/14/books/review/Kinsley-t.html?_r=2&pagewanted=print

[12] Greenspan, Alan (2007). The age of turbulence: adventures in a new world. pp. 70-73

[13] Benjamin, Matthew (2005). The Greenspan Legacy, USNews. p. 2

[14] Leonard, David (2012). Alan Greenspan on his FED legacy and the economy, business week. pp. 2-3

on he worked on election calculations.[15] Though, when he was asked to join the white house staff, he kindly declined, because he preferred his old job.

In the following period, until 1987, when he finally was elected to be the chairman at the Federal Reserve, he had various corporate director functions at for example: *Alcoa, Mobil, J.P. Morgan,* and several memberships with i.e. *Council on Foreign Relations,* and *The Group of 30.*[16]

[15]Ambrose, Stephen (1987). Nixon. New York: Simon & Schuster. p. 158.
[16]Greenspan, Alan (2007). The age of turbulence: adventures in a new world. pp. 89

FED

Alan Greenspan was nominated by *President Ronald Reagan,* as the successor of Mr. Volcker, as chairman of the board of governors of the Federal Reserve. Because he is fond of numbers, his period at the FED can be best described as 18, 5.55, 3, 2

18 is the number of years he was chairman of the board at the FED, being the second longest term for this position.

During this era, the unemployment rate was averaged on 5.55%. If we compare that to other years, before and after him, we see that in 18 years before him, the average percentile was 6.65%, so more than a 1% decrease. And after his period, this percentage was a stunning 8.1%.[17]

Also equally important there is the number 3, this stands for 3% inflation. Again, compared with the

---

[17] Bureau of labor statistics (2012).
http://www.bls.gov/news.release/empsit.nr0.htm

years before and after, it's a pretty good job, considering before him, it was 6.5%, and after him only a mere 1,4%. Then there is the most important of all, 2. During his period he had to cope with 2 recessions.[18]

Numbers don't tell all of course, but give a pretty good insight on his policies. The overall view of his was term was *risk-management*. He had to cope with several crises, and several to-be crises. But he did a fairly good job on managing the crises.

---

[18] Benjamin, Matthew (2005). The Greenspan Legacy.
www.usnews.com/usnews/news/articles/051024/24greenspan_p
rint.htm

Post-FED

Soon after the FED, Alan Greenspan started his economic consultancy firm again, and had several consultant positions at various companies. Some of them are PIMCo, Deutsche Bank, and Paulson.

He also wrote his memoir, and soon another book by him will be ready for the public as well.

He also received various and numerous merits, honors, and doctorates from various Universities all around the world.

2 ANALYSIS ON LEADERSHIP

There are many ways to define a leader or one's leadership capabilities, and even more sub routes so to speak, to define abilities or study one's leadership. Let us follow the framework provided in the book *by Laurie J. Mullins "Management & Organisational Behaviour"[19]*

Qualities or traits approach

The qualities or traits approach is following the *Great person theory of Leadership,* and is all about the person instead of the job.

As this approach assumes that leaders are born with a certain set of characteristics, let's look at certain characteristics of Alan Greenspan. One of the key elements he was born with is intelligence.

---

[19] Laurie J. Mullins (2012) Management & Organisational Behaviour, 9th ed. Prentice hall

His father was a stockbroker and market analyst at Wall Street, and once can assume that for those jobs you need some sort of intelligence.[20]

Further, you could say that for a stock broker, you need to have self-confidence, and although not shown in his early years, you could say that while at the FED and even before, on the Nixon campaign he is/was very self-confident, believing more in his own ideas, rather than ideas from Nixon, and that he even dared to challenge Nixon about those ideas. (Later on he was proven right)

Functional (or group) approach & action-centred

In contrast with the approach of the traits approach, the functional approach relies on the idea that one must have a certain set of skills, but that you

---

[20] New York Times: "Alan Greenspan, Andrea Mitchell" (http://www.nytimes.com/1997/04/06/style/alangreenspan-andrea-mitchell.html) April 06, 1997

can learn or develop those leadership skills.

Next to that, the principle of action-centered leadership revolves around the idea of what leaders do, in comparison with the needs of the task, the individual and the team.

In many opinions, while Alan was chairman of the FED, he did an excellent job, combining the different needs, and had some sort of equilibrium in place. As you look to the task needs, he certainly defined clear tasks, and had a good reviewing system in place to control quality and performance. If you look at the team needs, he had set standards, and everyone, or at least most of the employees, had great discipline in the work he was involved in. Lastly, if we check the individual needs, he could give appraisal for someone's work, and especially for the markets he wasn't an expert in, or parts he didn't quite understand, he had full admiration for those who did understand. At least, that is, according

12

to his own words, on various pages in his book.[21]

Leadership as a behavioral category

According to himself, he would like to restructure anything in numbers. His greatest concern at the FED, was that he wanted all information in crisp clear reports. His goal was the goal of the organization. We could derive from this that he likely would be in the form of Theory X, production centered supervision, initiating structure.

Styles of Leadership

Alan Greenspan shifted along various styles of leadership along his career. First (before FED) he had more of a dictator-alike autocratic style, then he shifted to a more laissez-faire style, and at the end of his career he moved to a democratic style.

---

[21] Greenspan, Alan (2007). The age of turbulence: adventures in a new world. pp. various

At his co-owned company, there was a clear line and distinction between the two CEOs. Everyone had to listen to him, and he could not accept any comments on his style of working. The overall perception was *"Don't ask, just do it"*

Later, when he increasingly became more important, and was influenced more by his dear friend Ayn Rand, he shifted to the genuine style or laissez-fair. Objectivism is a way of thinking that if you let everything go, and don't manage anything, everything will work out, thus the perfect environment of laissez-fair. Ultimately, during his terms at the FED, he moved slowly to the democratic style, trusting his group around him more and more, and accepted them as more or less equals.

If you would look at the continuum of behavior, you basically see the same. Mid-career he made a combination of consulting and selling. He first consulted a small group of intimates, and then "sells" it to the rest of the world.

Then later, one could see the similarities between his democratic style, and the "Join" style.

Situational approach and contingency models

There are many contingency models, of which 4 are a major model. Though, in my opinion they are very alike. The focus here, is on the Vroom and Yetton model, and will link that to the other models.

During the major time at the FED, Greenspan was a typical Consultative leader, and depending on the situation, sometimes more a C.II and sometimes more alike C.I.

It is commonly known that he consults a group of subordinates, and often also a group outside the FED, and then, after having seen a challenge from all sides, he made a decision, which of course, could or could not reflect ideas of someone else.

If we check then Fiedler's model, we see that being a good leader, having a structured task, and is the relationship moderately, brings us to option V.

If we lay it over the path-goal theory, than we see that he is a participative leader.

If we compare it to the situational leadership model from Hersey, we see again the participative leader, or the so called S3 type. It does not compare to the follower readiness however, because in my opinion they are more of an R4 type, or ultimately, a very strong R3.

This looks like his direct subordinates were able, willing and confident. Maybe though, they were not 100% confident after all.

Transformational Leadership

Greenspan is known most for his Transformational leadership. One of his key-elements is his superb capability of dealing with complex and uncertain situations. Along the line of duty, and years passing by, he managed to use this type of leadership and his intellect, to apply this to real world around him.

On top of that, he uses his experience, and that of others, to develop himself and others even further, but also to increase his decision making abilities even further.

For example, in one of his years, the city of NY faced serious bankruptcy. He, and perhaps his team, thought of a solution to please both sides; the troubled NYC, and the investors.

In other words, NYC could be bailed out, but investors or borrowers still could earn interest. This situation, and complex challenge or puzzle, he used many times after this point, but refined it every time.

Inspirational Leadership

Perhaps, inspirational or visionary leadership is an extension of the transformational leadership model. Possibly, this type of leadership is all about having a charismatic appearance, and having a strong vision. Greenspan had both. His vision was clear, e.g. a strong and good economy. But he was also a real charismatic person.

How else could one being admired by literally billions of people all around the globe, and react and on his speeches. Reaction on speeches is a bit strange, since he is a master of "FED-speak"

FED-speak is construction of sentences in such a way that it is incoherent, and could be interpreted in various ways. Greenspan uses this type of speak very often in speeches, and regardless of doing so, markets did react on his words, and thus meaning a lot listen or try to listen to him. For this kind of art, you have to be a charismatic person.

3 MANAGEMENT ELEMENTS

Alan Greenspan is not so much of a manager. He was of course "managing" the FED, but he is a manager because of the job - not so much for his skills.

Though, when following the managerial grid, you would say he is a mix of 2 styles or combinations. It changes back and forth, and depending on the situation, it looks like sometimes he preferred to be the "authority-compliance" manager, and on other occasions he was more of the "team manager".

When we have a look at the management systems, we see that actually he perused all 4 systems during his career. Being in the beginning of his work at the system 1 and 2 mode (the authoritative mode) and later shifted to the 3 and 4 type of system (the participative and consultative).

This we have seen at his leadership style as well in the previous chapter. The 3d model of managerial behavior looks a lot the same as other leadership models. In this case you could suggest that Greenspan is in the Integrated behavior style, having both a high orientation for tasks and for relationships.

4 CONCLUSION

Alan Greenspan, full of traits, and qualities, is a born leader, but perhaps not so much of a manager. He has his own strong vision, and is a charismatic person. He is thus an inspirational leader.

Next to that, he is learning from mistakes, from previous challenges, and from other markets. He uses that to develop himself, and others around him, and to combine all this in order to enhance future tasks. This makes him a strong transformational leader.

Further, he is participating in group sessions, and sometimes, depending on the situation, he consults others. By doing so, he can get a clear greater picture of the whole, and thus making him more decisive. Others may or may not influence his thoughts, which would always be the question. That makes him having the combination of C.I and C.II leadership styles.

Despite all these and other styles, he excels in transformational leadership. He certainly has all other traits making him an effective leader, and he should those as well, but you can clearly see he fits best in the role of transformational leader.

Having said that he is not much of a manager, is because although he is an mastermind on the area of economics, and he knows a lot from a lot of different subjects, he is more put in place as a chairman because all this and perhaps because of his leadership qualities, rather than because of his managerial qualities.

5 SOURCELIST

Martin, Justin. (Greenspan, The man behind money) 2000. Perseus. Cambridge, Massachusetts.

Greenspan, Alan (The age of turbulence: adventures in a new world) 2007. The Penguin Press, NY.

Modern Library, http://www.modernlibrary.com/top-100/100-best-novels/

Modern Library, http://www.modernlibrary.com/top-100/100-best-nonfiction/

NY Times, http://www.nytimes.com/2007/10/14/books/review/Kinsley-t.html?_r=2&pagewanted=print

Leonard, David (2012). Alan Greenspan on his FED legacyand the economy, businessweek. pp. 2-3

Ambrose, Stephen (1987). Nixon. New York: Simon & Schuster. p. 158.

Bureau of labor statistics (2012). http://www.bls.gov/news.release/empsit.nr0.htm

Benjamin, Matthew (2005). The Greenspan Legacy. www.usnews.com/usnews/news/articles/051024/24greenspan_print.htm

Laurie J. Mullins (2012) Management &
Organisational Behaviour, 9th ed. Prentice hall

New York Times: "Alan Greenspan, Andrea
Mitchell"
(http://www.nytimes.com/1997/04/06/style/alangree
nspan-andrea-mitchell.html) April 06, 1997

Hersey, Dr Paul. The Situational Leader. 1985
Warner Books, New York

Rasiel, Ethan M. The McKinsey Way. 2002
McGraw-Hill, New York

Binder, Alan & Reis, Ricardo. Understanding the
Greenspan Standard. 2005

The Economist, 2009. He Had the Power.
www.economist.com/blogs/freeexchange/2009/03/he
_had_the_power/print

The NY Times, 2007. Greenspan Shrugged.
www.nytimes.com/2007/10/14/books/review/Kinsle
y-t.html?_r=2&pagewanted=print

ABOUT THE AUTHOR

After high school, the author studied administration in Utrecht, The Netherlands, then the author studied International Business and Management in Amsterdam, The Netherlands, and Econometrics in Lisbon, Portugal. Now the author lives happily in the center of The Netherlands, and travels frequently around the globe for the day job.

From the same author the following books were published previously:

'Business Cycle Redefined'

'How to: Start a company with no funds?'

'Waste Management in the Health Sector - How to (re)solve it?'

'Recommendations & Solutions to shorten lead times in Health sector'

'The Fundamental Basics of International Product Trade'